Contributory Author
Brian Knapp, BSc, PhD
Art Director
Duncan McCrae, BSc
Special photography
Graham Servante
Special models
Tim Fulford, Head of CDT, Leighton Park School
Editorial consultants
Anna Grayson, Rita Owen
Science advisor
Jack Brettle, BSc, PhD, Chief Research Scientist,
Pilkington plc
Illustrators
Mark Franklin
Production controller
Gillian Gatehouse
Print consultants
Landmark Production Consultants Ltd
Printed and bound in Hong Kong

Designed and produced by
EARTHSCAPE EDITIONS,

First published in the USA in 1991 by
GROLIER EDUCATIONAL CORPORATION,
Sherman Turnpike, Danbury, CT 06816

Copyright © 1991
Atlantic Europe Publishing Company Ltd

Library of Congress #91–075970

Cataloging information may be obtained
directly from Grolier Educational Corp.

ISBN 0–7172–7170–6

In this book you will find some words that have been shown in **bold** type. There is a full explanation of each of these words on pages 46 and 47.

On many pages you will find experiments that you might like to try for yourself. They have been put in a colored box like this.

Acknowledgements
The publishers would like to thank the following:
Leighton Park School, Micklands County
Primary School, Redlands County Primary
School, Graham Gatehouse, Philippa Trounce,
The Royal Borough of Windsor and Maidenhead
and Tim Warr

Picture credits
t=top b= bottom l=left r=right

All photographs from the Earthscape Editions
photographic library except the following: Bruce
Coleman Ltd 17tr; Graham Gatehouse 11t;
ZEFA 17tl, 30/31, 32/33, 35

Contents

Introduction

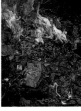

cans
page 32

fires
page 40

glass
page 34

wrappers
page 8

paper
page 24

Look around your room. How many of the things you see are more than a few years old? How many will still be in your room in a few years time?

Most people buy new things when the old ones get worn out or when a new style comes into fashion. Then they simply throw the old things away.

In this book we shall find out about waste – materials that we throw away. In our homes we have wastebaskets to store all the waste. In the street there are garbage cans to help us to keep public places tidy. There are street cleaners to clear up after less thoughtful people.

In the garden there may be a special place for vegetable waste – it's called a compost heap.

litter
page 10

steel
page 30

collecting
page 22

brushes
page 14

plastic
page 26

Because the collection of garbage is so well organized, we may not think about how wasteful we can be. We may not think about the amounts of valuable materials we throw out, or how difficult it is to cope with them. We only get a glimpse of the size of the problem if collections stop and garbage piles up on the streets.

Garbage can be valuable. Much of it can be used again. Unless we re-use more of our garbage we will run out of places to store it. Worse still, we will also run out of some of the materials we need to make new things.

In this book you can discover the fascinating story of garbage in any way you choose. Just turn to a page and begin your discoveries.

5

Made to throw away

We live in a world full of things to buy. We like to buy things that are fun and easy to use and colorful to look at.

The people who make our goods are happy to help. So most of the things we buy are made in large, colorful wrappings. They make buying more fun, but the wrappings are made to throw away.

Even the things we used are made to throw away. Here's why.

2% clothes

What a waste

A garbage can often contains glass bottles, paper wrappers and metal cans. Many people also throw out machines, food, timber, worn out clothes and even broken building blocks.

The numbers on this picture show you the percentages of each type of garbage in a 'typical' garbage can.

25% vegetable waste

10% glass

Mixed up

The picture to the right shows part of the inside of a computer. It is made of hundreds of parts and most of them are made of different materials. Ask a grown-up if there is an old machine you can help to take apart. Together carefully take out all the pieces and try to see what each piece is made of. Then sort the pieces into similar materials. How big is the pile of mixed materials?

Unmendable

Have a look at the things you use. Do you see any screws or clips that will let you get inside?

Most of the things we buy are finished by machines that leave everything sealed in tight. This is good while the things are working, but if something goes wrong it costs far more to repair than to replace. So when it goes wrong you have to throw it away.

Less bother with a disposable

Many things are made to be convenient to use.

Look at your pen. The chances are you cannot fill it up with ink once it is empty. Things like pens that are sealed up and made to be thrown away when they have been used for a short time are called **disposables**.

Many of our goods have to be disposable. The ink was put into the pens by a special machine. You could not do it for yourself.

15% ash, chemicals, **manufactured** goods

10% metals

30% paper and **packaging**

8% plastics

7

Taking off the wraps

Many things we buy are wrapped up in several ways. These wrappers each do a separate job, and together they are called packaging. Much packaging is made from paper, but plastic, glass, wood and metal are all used.

Packaging is essential. The problem is how best to re-use it.

This cosmetic pack has been packaged in clear plastic. It allows each item to be displayed without handling and it makes the pack look like better value for the money

Complicated wraps

The need for special packages is not always obvious. For example, if you look inside a box of ground coffee, you will see what appears to be an ordinary bag. But to keep the coffee fresh, clean and tasty, the metal foil bag has had to be coated with up to five special plastics.

The plastic bag is sealed to keep out moist air and germs. The bag also traps clean dry air. The bag is like a plastic bubble, helping to protect the contents from crushing

These cornflakes break up easily if crushed and they lose their crunchy texture and become soggy if exposed to the air. Because they are food, cornflakes must also be protected from harmful germs in the air

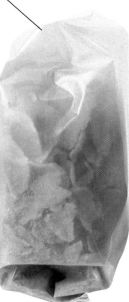

Packages that sell

Packaging is important to keep goods clean, fresh and easy to move about. But many packs are also designed to make the goods they contain sell better.

The makers want the package to look like a better value or to be easily seen on a shelf. This is why even small items like sweets are packaged in colorful wrappers.

Don't throw it away

Paper and cardboard can't easily be sorted by machine, so it is best to sort it yourself and keep it in bundles. There are many charities that collect old paper and cardboard.

Packs unlimited

Find some items that you have bought from the stores. Choose ones that use paper or cardboard for wrappers.

Unpack them carefully and spread the unwanted packaging out on the floor. Place all the packaging side by side, biggest at one end, smallest at the other.

What is the biggest piece of packaging you can find? Did the biggest packs match to the largest contents? If not, what was the purpose of the large packs? What was the purpose of the *shape* of the pack?

The carton carries the name of the cornflakes and makes an awkward-shaped bag into a **rectangular** shape that will pack together for easy transportation and be easy to stack on shelves

This outer carton and plastic wrap groups the product into sizes that are economical to move about. Most of the cardboard is made from **recycled** paper

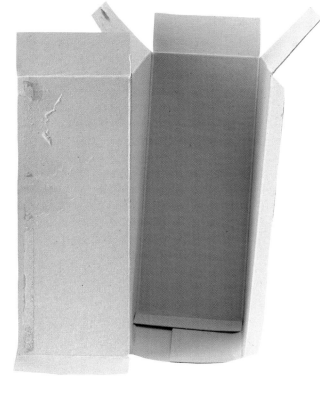

Follow the litter trail . . .

Litter is the name given to materials thrown away in public places. It contains a wide variety of materials from paper to metal cans.

Most litter is produced by the things people throw away while walking along. The more we collect, the better our world.

When litter is left
When people have picnics they sometimes leave their litter strewn on the ground. Unsightly litter can spoil a pleasant walk.

Litter is much more difficult to pick up after a few days. The paper may be wet and too weak to be moved and things can get scattered around by animals as they search for left-over bits of food.

Spot the litter level
Litter can build up very quickly at places where there are many people. Sports arenas can have thousands of people packed together for hours. At train stations and bus stops people have to stand waiting. In busy streets people often eat as they move from shop to shop.

Can you think of any other places where litter is common? Look out for litter trails on your way to and from school.

Caution:
If you collect litter, always use special tools, protective gloves and a plastic bag for hygiene reasons

Litter left under seats in a popular tourist spot

Tidy town

How tidy is your town? Is it covered with litter or are the streets clean?

Make a check on the garbage cans. Are they kept empty or do they spill over? Or do people simply walk by without using them?

If people do not seem to care enough, design a poster that you think would make them care more.

Keep a check on litter

Try to find out how litter changes in an area near you.

Find a garbage can in a street and use it as a marker. Now pace your way along the street.

As you go count the number of pieces of litter you find. You may even want to keep a record of what each piece of litter was made of.

You can make a chart of the pieces of litter and compare them with the distance from the garbage can.

11

Giving litter a good home

Wastebaskets are very common. But do they all do a good job?

Each wastebasket has to be sturdy and easy to keep clean. It also has to be placed so it is easy to use. Above all it has to be shaped so that people can throw their litter away without difficulty.

The best way to find out about wastebaskets is to make one yourself – from litter naturally!

Litter for litter
Papier mache means *paper pulp*. It is hard and strong when dry.

To make a papier mache wastebasket, first make the shape, or form, you want out of cardboard or use a ready-made shape such as a bucket.

Wrap a sheet of paper around the shape and stick it to itself with tape. Make a base in the same way as shown in this picture.

Use some paper strips (or perhaps pieces of paper litter) and wallpaper paste to stick strip after strip until you have built up a layer which everywhere is several strips thick.

When the paste has dried, ease the papier mache off the form.

Bucket used as form

Base

A finished wastebasket

Blending in

Choose a suitable color for painting your wastebasket. Should it be brown, so that it blends into the street colors, or orange so it is easy to see? Or perhaps it should be some other color such as green for a country park or yellow for a beach?   Or should it have pasted pieces of litter on the outside?

Bear's thinking about

This is a garbage can that has been designed for a place where forest bears are common. It is quite unlike normal garbage cans – it has been made very difficult to get in to! If a bear got to this garbage it would make a dreadful mess.

This garbage can would not score well in a litterball competition, but it is widely used outdoors. Can you think why?

Litter ball

One way to test a wastebasket is to make a game of litter ball. Crumple a piece of paper into a tight ball. Now try to throw the litter ball into the wastebasket.

   How far away can you go and still get your ball in the wastebasket each time? Give a wastebasket a score. If you can stand two feet from the wastebasket and get your litter ball in first time award 1 litter ball point.

   Now stand three feet away and try again. If you can get the ball in give two litter ball points. Give more points the further away you can stand.

Sweeping up

Sometimes we can't help leaving waste. For example, cars leave tiny pieces of tire rubber on the road as they travel along and you leave small pieces of shoe leather or rubber on the street as you walk.

Nature sheds its own form of waste. A strong wind will swirl leaves about or blow soil onto the streets and into houses.

Cleaning up all these tiny pieces of waste can be a difficult job.

Street cleaning machines

Street cleaning machines may look strange but they have been designed to do a special job. The big brushes at the front swirl round, loosen stubborn dirt and sweep the garbage towards the center of the machine.

Underneath the machine is a big vacuum cleaner which sucks the dirt and waste into the 'bag'. The bag is the big box behind the driver's cab. It allows the machine to work for a long time before the bag needs emptying.

Vacuum cleaning

One of the best ways to clean up small pieces of waste is with a vacuum cleaner.

Have a look at the contents of a vacuum cleaner bag. Can you see what is the most common type of waste you leave about the house? Is there any way you could have stopped it? What can you usefully do with this waste?

Circular brushes: a new one on the left, one that has been used for a few weeks on the right

Metal wires will even get chewing gum off the road surface!

Water cleaning power

Ask a grown-up to connect the hose and turn it on. Hold your thumb slightly over the end of the hose and see the water turn into a fan shape. Try cleaning an area of concrete such as a patio or drive using the force of the water. Decide which shape of water fan works best.

Hands on cleaning

The simplest way to clean the streets is with a hand brush. Hand sweeping is useful in places which are awkward to clean. But a lot of people will be needed to clean a city by hand sweeping, and most of it is not very pleasant work.

Find out about street sweeping. Use a stiff brush and find out how much pavement you can clean in five minutes. How much pavement could you sweep in a day? Is it tiring or easy work? Is sweeping an effective way of cleaning?

If this boy wanted to clean the streets as well as the machines, this is what he would need

Out of sight?

Some garbage can be burned, some can be re-used. But at the end of the day there will always be some garbage left over. This is the material that has to be buried in huge pits.

Old **quarries** can often be used as sites for garbage. The problem in the future will be what to do when all the quarries are full.

Eating up space

What would you do with a pile of garbage? It contains many things that cannot easily be re-used.

Even home produced garbage takes up a lot of space as you can see by looking at your own garbage cans. Think of the problems in coping with the waste from a big city.

This is a garbage truck. It is designed to collect garbage from schools, offices and other large producers. The garbage can is automatically lifted and the contents tipped into the truck. Special crushers in the truck then compress the garbage

B159 FTF

Waste risk

Waste left lying around can be a risk to health as well as being unsightly. Rats, flies and other creatures that carry disease are quickly attracted to piles of garbage. It is therefore important to deal with garbage as soon as possible.

Most garbage is heavy and awkward to handle even for special machines

The world's biggest dump

The largest garbage dump – called a **landfill site** – in the world is a place known as Fresh Kills, Staten Island New York. It covers an area of 3 square miles. Every hour 1000 tons of garbage are brought to the dump.

By the end of the century Fresh Kills will no longer be a pit. Instead it will be about the height of a 50 story building. It will be one of the largest man-made mountains in the world – full of garbage.

Want not, waste a lot

If someone asked you to wear someone else's old clothes what would you do? If you were given a pair of shoes made from old tires what would you think? If you were asked to take your soft drink bottle back to get it refilled, would you bother?

The chances are you would be horrified if any of these things happened. This is because we are used to getting new things to wear. And we are used to buying clean, well wrapped, things that are fun to buy and exciting to look at. But others are not so lucky.

Money from waste
In these dumps children are collecting old bottles and cans so they can sell them again. They have to sift over a mountain of garbage. It is unpleasant work and they can catch diseases from the refuse. But they do it every day because this is how they help their families make enough money to survive. Nothing goes to waste here.

Children having a break from sorting garbage at Mexico City, Mexico

They don't throw it away!

A want not world is one that is short of money. All the people on this page are short of money. People like this make up three-quarters of all the people in the world. This means they have to look around to find new ways of using old things.

The boy is carrying water to his home in old plastic containers that once held something else. He is using a wheelbarrow made out of planks of wood that have been tied together. And the wheel is roughly cut from another piece of wood. He is wearing shoes that were once tires. And he has not thrown away his clothes just because they have started to wear out.

An attractive toy made from scrap wire, Kenya

What do you waste?

Most of us are fortunate not to be poor. But we should still be careful not to waste our world.

Find out how much waste you make every day. Keep a diary of how many wrappers you throw away, how many cans or bottles you throw into the garbage. Ask your parents to show you what they have thrown away during the day. The chances are it's a lot more than you think.

Sandals made from old tires, Zambia

Sorting with science

Think of all the materials that are mixed up in a garbage can. None of it can be useful when its all mixed up.

But how can you sort it out easily? Here are some ideas on how to sort with science.

Sorting order

The secret to good sorting is to choose the right order of operations. This will allow the greatest number of materials to be saved and re-used.

Steel can easily be taken out with a magnet, so this can be done first. Remember that burning is a last resort because it destroys many materials.

Put some garbage onto a garden sieve and shake it about. Can you sort by size?

Use a hair dryer to blow a wind over some of the garbage. Can you sort it with wind?

Put some nails in a small pile of garden soil. Use a small magnet and move it about in the soil. Can you sort with magnetism?

Hand treatment

Using your science have you been able to sort glass, paper or clothes from the rest of the garbage and still leave them useful for re-use?

Our science will not easily sort these items, so if we want to save and re-use them we have to sort them by hand.

Put a handful of garbage in a bowl of water. Can you see how to sort with water?

Look inside the wastebasket. Has shaking mixed the garbage or has it helped to sort it? Can you see what is common about the materials on the top and what is common about the materials in the bottom?

Caution
You should only handle 'clean' garbage

Let's give a hand

Garbage is too valuable to throw away. Our sanitation departments try to rescue as much as possible. But their job would be more efficient if we all helped to sort the garbage first. Here are some common ways of sorting in the home.

Paper piles
Paper is made from many different materials. Shiny papers have clay in them. They are best kept separate from newspapers. Cardboard is made differently again and is best kept in its own pile.

Food containers
When rotting food gets mixed up with other garbage it makes sorting almost impossible. It also attracts **vermin** and can spread disease. Unwanted food is far better kept in an old food container and then used to make compost.

Wherever you see this international symbol it tells you that people are helping to recycle materials

No go

People have learned the trick of putting things together quickly. But we still have to learn how to make things that will also come apart easily and quickly so they can be mended, or **reconditioned,** or the pieces used again or recycled.

This means that many things you have no use for cannot easily be sorted into piles. Radios, TVs and other electronics come into this category. Until people find quick ways of re-using them, they will unfortunately have to be thrown away.

Bottle depots

Glass can be dangerous if it is simply left around because it is easily broken. And it is not easy to sort it by machine. It is even harder to sort all the different colors of glass. To make most use of the glass it therefore needs to be sorted by color. This is why bottle depots are needed.

Glass is heavy. Have you noticed how the bottle depot is designed to be lifted on to the back of a truck and exchanged with an empty one? This saves time and effort.

23

<u>Ne</u>w paper from old

Make recycled paper
The strength of paper comes from tiny fibers of plant **cellulose**. But when used paper is made wet the fibers swell and the bonds between them weaken. Then they can be taken apart and made into new paper.

Paper is one of the most common materials. It is used for this book, for your exercise books, for newspapers, as wrappers, wallpaper and many other things. It is even used to make the wood-like surface of some furniture.

Our needs for paper are so great that millions of trees must be cut down each year. Every re-used sheet of paper is good news for a live tree somewhere in the world.

1. To recycle your own paper ask a grown-up to help you to make two square frames like the ones shown here. They should be about the size of this book and fixed firmly with nails and glue.

On one of the frames stretch and fix some fine fabric such as old net curtain

2. Tear up some white paper into small pieces and put it into a bowl with water. When it has soaked, mash it up with a whisk or fork. Drain off any excess water. You should aim to get a mixture like thick soup. This makes the **pulp**.

If you want scented paper now is the time to mix in some mashed up scented plant leaves. If you want to see the plant remains in the finished paper, don't mash them up

24

3. Slide the frames into the pulp with the net frame underneath. Lift out the frames while shaking gently side to side. The aim is to get an even thickness of paper on the net

4. Put a piece of paper towel on a board. Take off the top pulp frame and turn the lower frame over so the layer of pulp goes down onto the paper towel. Rub the net so the pulp is pressed onto the towel, then lift the net and frame away, leaving the pulp on the towel

5. Put another towel on the pulp, then make another sheet of paper and put it on the towel. Repeat until you have several sheets. Then put a board on top and stand on the board to squeeze out the water. The sheets can now be separated carefully and left to dry

It's a plastic world

Plastic is very useful because it will mold easily into complicated shapes, it can be very strong and tough, and it will not rust or rot in the rain.

But the very properties that make it useful also make it one of the most difficult materials to recycle. Nevertheless, it can often be re-used. In the future new forms of plastic will be recycled.

Plastic, a wonder material?
Plastic is the name given to a large group of man-made materials that are easily molded into new shapes using heat and pressure.

Plastic can be made from oil, coal, gas, wood, and some kinds of plants. There are now hundreds of different sorts of plastic, each doing a useful job and many doing jobs that could be done no other way.

Hamburger seed tray
Hamburger boxes can be used for many things. One idea is to use them as seed trays. First make a couple of small drain holes in the box base. Then plant some cress seeds. Cress just needs damp tissue paper to grown on as shown here.

Close the lid to keep the moisture inside. Check each day to see when the seeds have **germinated**. As soon as they pop through, leave the lid open.

Will hamburger seed trays germinate seeds far faster than normal seed trays? Why not make a test to find out?

Don't throw it away

The world's oil **reserves** will not last forever. It is important to use them carefully. In the future scientists will probably be able to make many plastic things from plants. These plastics will also probably rot naturally away when they are no longer needed.

It is important to 'buy time' until this can come about. One easy way is to buy strong plastic shopping bags and use them time after time. Refuse to have goods wrapped in plastic if they don't need to be wrapped. Just pop them into your own bag.

This wire is covered with a coat of plastic. Plastic does not allow electricity to pass through it and so it is used to insulate the wires in a cable. For the same reason is also used for plugs and sockets and for the cases of electrical **appliances**

Insulating boxes

The hamburger box is a made specially to be strong. It must also be an **insulating** material, that is it must keep the heat in until people have time to eat their food.

To do these jobs, the material used for the packs is a special type of plastic, or foam, that has been made into a froth before it set hard.

Tires

Tires are made from man-made, or synthetic, rubber. However, this hard-wearing material is now being made in vast quantities. One tire is used up for every two people each year.

Waste tire materials can catch fire and release poisonous chemicals. One way to deal with them is to grind them into powder and then add the powder to road materials to give better grip. Most are just buried.

Lurking poisons

You may think that you are living in a house, but it is more like a chemical laboratory. Everywhere around you there are chemicals.

Chemicals have particular jobs to do around the house. But many are also poisonous and can catch fire. You need to be very careful before you decide to throw them away.

Leaving well alone

Chemicals are designed for particular jobs. They may also be dangerous in other situations. Many glues, for example, give off a gas which will catch fire and which can explode.

This is the reason that cans and bottles that contained chemicals should never be burned on a fire. They should be set to one side so the garbage collectors can deal with them properly.

Even traces of some chemicals can be dangerous, especially if they are drunk. This is why bottles and jars that have been used for chemicals should never be rinsed and reused for food or drink. They should always be disposed of in a special recycling center.

Aerosols

Aerosols are cans of liquids under pressure. Things like insect sprays and car paint sprays are aerosols.

The chemicals used in aerosols are often harmful and should not be breathed in. But most important of all, the cans have pressurized gas inside them even when they are 'empty' and they no longer serve a useful purpose. Many of the gases will explode if the cans are put on a fire or if the cans are crushed.

Caution
Always take warning labels seriously

Harmful

Highly flammable

Don't pour it away

It is very difficult to dispose of chemicals. Many people think that the safest thing to do is to pour unwanted chemicals onto soil. Usually this will kill all soil animals and poison the plants.

Other people think the best thing to do is to pour the chemicals down the drains. Every day a huge chemical **cocktail** enters the drains. It makes dealing with waste water very much more expensive and dangerous. In the long run this costs us all money. And of the drains accidentally overflow into rivers all the life in the river can be killed.

The only sensible thing is to seal the containers and put them out for the garbage collectors to deal with properly.

Caution
Never try to save space by putting used chemicals together in one container. You could cause an explosion, a fire, or produce fumes that could kill

Chemical paste fills most of the space inside the case

Batteries

Batteries are made from many poisonous and rare substances. They are not good things to throw away. If they are put on a fire they could also explode. If they rot in a waste heap they could leak poisonous chemicals.

If batteries are thrown away the precious metals inside are simply wasted and more of the Earth has to be dug up to find new sources. So although batteries are tiny, they contain important re-usable materials. You may find a battery dump near you.

Steel appeal

Our world depends on metals: our cars have metal bodies and engines and our skyscrapers have metal frames; we go over metal bridges and we drink from metal cans. All of the wires that connect electrical devices are made of metal; we cook in metal pans and use metal knives and forks.

If metal objects are simply thrown out they look unsightly and waste valuable resources.

Scrap but not scrapped

Scrap is the name given to metal goods that are no longer needed.

A scrap yard is a place where everything is sorted and saved if at all possible. Most of the recycled material is steel.

The cars shown in this picture have been stripped down and the bodies squashed to the size of large biscuit tins. They make up the strange shapes in the pile on the right. This makes it easier to transport the steel back to the steel works for recycling.

Metal with a message

This is a young person's idea of how to use the parts for a steel engine in a sculpture. It shows just how many parts go to make up a machine and just how much useful scrap there is to recycle.

Try to find parts of old machines. Perhaps you could visit a junk yard with a grown-up. Make a sculpture at school to illustrate how important steel recycling is.

Unseen metals

Metals are mainly found in rocks. A natural material with useful metals in it is called an **ore**. Iron is the most common metal used today.

Turning ore into metal can only be done in a very hot furnace. It is a skilled process that uses a lot of energy.

Can recycle

One of the largest uses of steel and aluminium is in 'tin' cans. Nearly all food cans are made of steel, most soft drink cans are made of aluminum. The populations of every major country in the world *each* throw out *billions* of cans a year. All may be recycled.

These cans have been left scattered on a desert. They are unsightly and they will not rot away quickly. In a desert they may last for thousands of years, but in any environment they are ugly

In Africa there are not many places for recycling cans in furnaces. But people still find ways of re-using them. Here a tomato can is used as a lamp

New cans from old

Some metals are used and then discarded quite quickly. For example, very large amounts of aluminum are used to make the cans that hold soft drinks. It makes sense to collect the old cans and use them again.

Making a new can from an old one always uses a lot less energy that getting new metal from ore. Less than a twentieth of the energy is needed to make a can from recycled cans that from the aluminum ore.

The first step to help recycling is to crush a can to reduce its bulk

Strong glass

Glass is good for packaging because it is strong, cheap to make and, when properly sealed, it keeps germs at bay.

Glass can be used for windows and windshields, it can be made into fiberglass and used to make bodywork. Long threads of glass (called optical fibers) can even be used to send telephone and television signals.

Designed for survival
The people who design the bottles and jars we use have to be careful to make them strong. The strongest shape is round, and this is why most glass containers are shaped like tubes.

Good storage

Glass is good for storing all kinds of things because it will not rot, it will only melt at very high temperatures, it keeps its shape, it has a smooth surface and is easy to clean. You can also easily see what is inside a glass container.

With all these advantages, jars and bottles can be used lots of times. This is the reason most of them have screw caps.

Jars with new uses

Many people make collections of empty jars and bottles. Some old ones are very valuable collector's items. But even ordinary bottles can be used for new purposes. This is easiest with screw-top jars that have wide necks.

Molten glass tubing being made in a factory

Don't throw it away

Glass is made from sand. First the sand is heated in a furnace until it melts. The molten sand – glass – is then squeezed into jar or bottle-shaped molds and left to cool.

Sand is very plentiful on Earth. It makes many of the rocks of the ground and the sand on the beach. But taking sand leaves huge holes in the ground. Why spoil more countryside when there is already enough glass if it is re-used?

About a tenth of everything we throw away is made of glass. Most of it can be re-used.

It is easy to put glass into a bottle depot like the one shown on page 23.

Good foundations

Building blocks and concrete are useful materials because they stand up to the weather, they are hard and strong, and they can be made into many different shapes.

Building blocks are made from clay that has been baked in a furnace, or from concrete (a mixture of sand, stones and cement). Cement is chalk and clay that have been baked and ground to a powder.

Billions of building blocks are made each year and millions of tons of concrete are mixed. Fortunately, both blocks and concrete can easily be re-used in the foundations of new buildings.

Make a rockery

A garden rockery is a good place to use rubble. All the odd shapes and sizes make the rockery look more interesting.

You may have room for a small rockery in your garden. To make a rockery you need some large pieces of clean building block or concrete rubble. Start with a wide base and get narrower as you pile the rubble higher. This will make a stable shape.

Between each piece of rubble put some soil so plants will have a place to grow. The **perennial** plants shown here will thrive all year and will tolerate dry, hot weather or cold. Many **annual** plants, such as nasturtiums, thrive on poor rocky soil. They will cover your rockery with brilliant orange flowers all summer.

A rockery

Waste building materials

Don't throw it away

Most old building materials are buried out of sight. The majority are used to make foundations for new buildings and roads.

First the rubble – called hard-core – is spread onto the site and then it is hammered down to make a firm foundation. Then it can be covered over with new concrete.

Using a hard-core of old building materials not only recycles unwanted and bulky rubble, it also reduces the amount of new blocks and concrete that have to be made. This saves digging up so much new countryside.

This castle looks as though it may have fallen into disrepair because of the weather. But the blocks have hardly weathered at all. Instead, they have been put to good use and recycled – they make up the walls of the houses seen in the foreground

This ancient monument is Quatab Minar in India. Built of clay **bricks** hundreds of years ago, it has hardly been scarred by the weather

Flexible wood

Wood is strong and light weight. It will bend before it breaks. It has been used by people for thousands of years to make homes and tools, tables and chairs, fences and gates. It can often be re-used with a little thought.

Chips to walk on

Most of the wood we use has been sawn into planks or other shapes. During the sawing a lot of wood has to be wasted. But the wasted wood can be used to make boards. Look at this chipboard. It is simply unwanted chippings that have been glued together and then pressed into a sheet. It can now be used to make floorboards or roofing sheets, cupboards and even table tops.

Wood is very fibrous and it is often ripped up into long splinters or 'chips' when trees are cut up for planks and other finished shapes. Here is a pile of 'chips' similar to those used to make the chipboard sheet shown below

This beautiful model is made from scraps of wood that might otherwise have been thrown away

Weed stoppers

When trees are sawn up for timber the bark is left over. Chipped up and spread over the soil, it gives a cover which keeps in the moisture and stops weeds growing. Look for forest bark chips in parks and near offices where people have little time for maintenance.

Forest bark chips

Old planks into new storage units

To make storage units for games and models, or bookcases all you need are some used building blocks and used planks of wood about the same width as the longest side of the blocks.

After you have placed two blocks for the feet and laid the first plank, test the board to see if it will sag when you press down firmly on the center. If it does then you need a block under the middle of the board as well.

Continue to place boards and blocks until you have made the bookcase the height you want it, but remember it will not be safe to go higher than three feet.

Don't throw it away

If you throw wood away it *could* rot down and make material for new trees to grow. Unfortunately this doesn't happen in much of the world. Many trees are cut and then shipped overseas. They never get replanted.

Re-using **hardwood** is especially important because it helps to protect the world's rainforests.

Don't throw the heat away

This is a specially designed wood stove. It burns wood more efficiently than an open fire

Heat energy is one of the easiest things to get from garbage. Over three quarters of everything we throw away can be burned. Burned garbage gives out a third as much heat energy as the same amount of coal.

Of course, the best thing to do with waste is to recycle it, but if it is very mixed up and can't be sorted, don't throw it away, burn it.

Up in smoke
Bonfires are an easy, but not very useful, or legal way to get rid of garbage. A huge pile of unwanted material can be turned into a small pile of ash very quickly. This happens because burning turns the garbage into different substances.

The smoke you see during a fire gives a clue to what is happening. The fire heats up the garbage until it turns into gases. Most of the gases are invisible. The smoke is made of tiny pieces of burnt garbage floating up with the hot gases.

Using heat energy

Fire is a good way to cook food or to boil a kettle. By cooking, you give some of the heat from the fire to the food or the water. Late in the evening you may also warm yourself by the fire. In this way you exchange the heat of the fire to do something useful.

We can turn garbage into useful heat by burning it in a furnace to make water turn to steam.

Steam is very useful for making machines work, and the steam from garbage furnaces can be used to make electricity which we can use in our homes.

Many people in poorer countries rely on wood or animal dung as their main fuel supply. This man is using cattle dung because he cannot afford any other source of fuel.

Burning dung is especially wasteful because the nutrients in the dung should be used as fertilizers on the fields and not sent up with the smoke.

Many poor people lose out in two ways. First they throw their fertilizer away. Second, the open fires they use for cooking are very inefficient and much of the precious heat is wasted

Matches to ashes

Get a grown up to light a match and place it on a saucer. When the match has burned away to ash place a new match by the side of the ash. Can you work out how much of the wood has been turned into gases and gone up as smoke?

Heaps of good news

Have you noticed how gardeners collect the dead leaves, stalks and roots in the Autumn?

Dead plants may look useless, but stored inside them are all the foods that next year's plants will need to grow. Releasing the foods – called **nutrients** – and re-using them is the job of lots of tiny animals that live in the soil.

Well decomposed leaves

The secret world of the compost heap
To make the work of the soil animals faster, gardeners pile up the plant garbage into special heaps called compost heaps.

A compost heap is a warm place where tiny animals thrive. As they grow, they eat up the dead plants and turn them into compost. When this is spread onto the garden soil it will give the goodness that the growing plants need.

Nature's silent work

Nothing is ever wasted by nature. Nature's compost heaps are all around you. Walk beneath a tree and see the layers of fallen leaves on the ground. Very carefully pick the surface leaves away and you will see partly rotted leaves below. Further down the leaves are even more rotted.

Leaves near the surface

Grow your own molds

Natural decay – we call it rotting – happens everywhere. It will happen in your garbage can if you leave old food there for too long. The cause is tiny **bacteria** and **fungi** that are too small to see.

When they have been working for a few days you can easily tell because the food gives off bad smelling gases and begins to get covered in green and grey patches called mold. The smell and look of food is the way we can tell that it is bad. This lemon shows the effect well.

Rotting needs air and moisture. You can test this for yourself using a piece of dry bread and a piece of moist bread.

Put each piece on a saucer on the window ledge. Keep one piece moist by adding some drops of water whenever it looks like drying out.

In a day or two a greenish mold - a type of fungus - will form on one sample. Which one do you think it will be?

This lemon shows how fungi grow on the surface as it rots. You can clearly see the green mould

Smells useful

Farmers have lots of wastes: dung from their animals and old plants after harvest. When organic material is available on a big scale it can be used for more than just compost.

As the food rots, or decays, it gives off gases which are detected by our noses. We call them smells.

Gases such as methane are useful if they can be trapped. They can be used to cook food and heat homes. This is especially useful to people in poorer parts of the world.

This is how the bag looks a week after the experiment has begun

This is how the bag looks at the start of the experiment

See the gas

You can see the gas produced by rotting vegetables if you put some old vegetable peelings in an old jar until it is three quarters full.

Add some water and then pull the open end of a plastic bag over the neck of the bottle and tie it on tightly with sticky tape to make an air-tight seal. To make the process faster you could add some yeast as used for wine-making. Yeast is a fungus.

Now you have made your own digester. Watch how the digestion takes place.

This is a traditional wood stove

Digesting biologically

In many parts of the world people already know what to do with their solid waste such as animal dung and waste food: dig a big pit, throw it in and stand back and wait for the natural bugs to **ferment** it. (You can find out how this works on page 42 because it is the same process as a compost heap).

The waste composts in specially lined and covered pits. They are like cooking pots with a lid. When the waste is shovelled in, normal decay causes it to heat up and release methane. The methane is trapped in the top of the pot until it is needed. Then it is simply fed through pipes to homes for heat and light.

Don't throw it away

People who digest their garbage biologically save space and trouble and get a free gas supply. They also get a free bonus. When the digested material is taken from the pot it is high grade and sterile compost: just right for putting back on the fields.

Plants need foodstuffs to grow. And the best fertilizers are those made naturally.

This man is cooking on a gas stove. It is a faster way of cooking than using wood

The large concrete structure is the gas-producing vessel. The pipe on the left leads to a house

New words

annual
a plant that grows, flowers, sets seed and dies in a year

appliance
any machine that has been made to do a particular job. It is normally made of many parts. A washing machine or a fridge are examples of large kitchen appliances

bacteria
microscopically small organisms that break down, or decompose, tissue. As they do this they release gases

bricks
a special form of clay building block found widely in the world. Some bricks have specially shaped dents in their faces to take cement, others have plain faces. Bricks are about a quarter the size of concrete building blocks

cellulose
a natural material that makes up the bulk of plant tissues. Cellulose often forms into tiny strings, or fibers

cocktail
a mixture of a range of different liquids

disposable
an object or appliance that cannot be repaired once it has worn out or become broken. Many of the components of electronic machines such as computers use disposable parts, but most ball point pens cannot be refilled and these are therefore also disposable

ferment
the process of rotting through the action of bacteria and fungi

fungi
microscopically small plants that cause dead tissue to rot

germinated
when seeds sprout into life they are said to have germinated

hardwood
hardwood trees have trunks with very closely packed fibers. This makes the wood dense and hard. Hardwoods are particularly useful for furniture and buildings because they do not easily rot or take up water. Hardwood trees grow very slowly and they are therefore hard to replace

insulate
an insulation is a covering of material that is designed to keep heat or electricity in or out. Insulation is used in the walls of many houses to keep them at a more even temperature, and to save the energy that would be needed for either heating or air conditioning. Plastic insulation is used to protect electrical cables

landfill
the name give to garbage that is dumped in an open pit, such as a disused quarry

manufactured goods
any objects that have been made by machine. Most manufactured goods are designed to be easy to make and to assemble. Normally they are a mixture of several types of materials. This makes them very difficult to recycle

nutrients
the chemicals that are released as dead tissue rots and which can be used by growing plants and animals to build new tissue

ore
any rock that contains useful amounts of metal. Most metals are extracted from their ores by heating in a furnace

perennial
a plant that lives for many years

pulp
the name given to the mashed up fibers of wood or recycled paper. Most pulp made in a factory has been through many chemical stages to get it to an even texture and a desired color

quarry
any large pit in solid rock that has been made by people searching for resources in the ground. Chalk, stone and metal ore quarries make some of the world's larges sites for garbage

reconditioned
a machine that has been reconditioned is one where the worn out parts have been replaced. Reconditioning equipment gives a new lease of life and is cheaper than replacing the whole machine

rectangular
the name for any block-shaped object. All the angles in a rectangular block are right angles

recycle
recycling refers to the way people can reuse materials to make new and useful products from old and worn out ones

reserves
the amount of material left in the Earth and which can be extracted by pumping or mining. The amount of reserves often gets larger as people find new ways to extract the desired material

vermin
any creature that may carry disease and which is seen as a pest. Very often it refers to rodents such as rats and mice

Index